100

CREATIVE THINKING TECHNIQUES

MONALISA PATNAIK

Dedication

For my beloved husband Uday and my precious daughter Trishika. This book is dedicated to you both, with great gratitude and love.

Acknowledgement

I AM PROFOUNDLY GRATEFUL to everyone who contributed to the creation of this book, ***100 Creative Thinking Techniques***. Writing a book is a collaborative effort, and I extend my heartfelt appreciation to those who played a pivotal role in making this project a reality.

First and foremost, I express my deepest gratitude to Manisha Panda, whose unwavering support, insightful feedback, and encouragement fuelled my creative journey. Your dedication to this project has been invaluable, and I am fortunate to have had you as a reviewer.

I am indebted to my family and friends for their patience, encouragement, and understanding throughout this process. Your belief in me sustained my spirit during the highs and lows of writing.

To the readers, your curiosity and open-mindedness are the catalysts that drive the purpose of this book. Thank you for embarking on this intellectual journey with me.

Lastly, I dedicate this work to Mr. Som Bathla, whose influence and inspiration permeate these pages.

Thank you all for being an integral part of this creative endeavor.

Cheers

The Purpose of the Book

100 **CREATIVE THINKING TECHNIQUES** is an indispensable guide for people from all walks of life, including entrepreneurs, students, professionals, and homemakers. The book is designed to overcome conventional thinking patterns and inspire a transformative mindset that can be applied to various aspects of daily life.

The aim of this book is twofold: First, it aims to encourage creativity and innovation by presenting a curated collection of 100 unconventional ideas, and second, it aims to provide practical insights into how these ideas can be implemented in the real world. It emphasizes the importance of thinking beyond traditional boundaries, fostering a culture of continuous improvement, and embracing change as a catalyst for personal and professional growth.

For entrepreneurs, the book offers imaginative strategies to break through market norms and foster the spirit of innovation that is critical to staying ahead of the competition. For students, it is a valuable resource to improve their critical thinking and problem-solving skills and prepare them for the challenges of a dynamic future. Professionals can apply the principles to increase their productivity, approach problem-solving creatively, and make their careers adaptable.

Stay-at-home moms and dads can also benefit, as the book encourages an imaginative and innovative approach to managing daily tasks and responsibilities. With practical insights and actionable ideas, *Revolutionizing Ideas* aims to empower people in a variety of fields to develop creativity, cultivate a forward-thinking mindset, and thrive in an ever-evolving world.

Preface

ONCE UPON A TIME, there was a young explorer named Aarav who lived in the vibrant city of Mumbai. Every morning, Aarav walked through the busy streets, following the same routine and longing for something beyond the ordinary. But the lure of the familiar never left him until a spark of curiosity flared up in him.

In the heart of the city, Aarav's morning rituals took place in the warmth of a traditional Indian home. Inspired by the rich heritage of his culture, Aarav decided to add a touch of creativity to his daily routine. Sunrise greeted Aarav 30 minutes earlier than the sun, bringing with it a refreshing energy that set the tone for the day.

The cozy corner of Aarav's home transformed into a sanctuary of mindfulness. Against a backdrop of soft sitar melodies, Aarav began his day with a few minutes of meditation, allowing the rich tapestry of Indian spirituality to fill every moment with calm and meaning.

As the first rays of sunlight lit up the city, Aarav, driven by his spirit of discovery, decided to change his route. The familiar streets of Mumbai gave way to hidden alleys and vibrant markets, and every corner revealed a new facet of the city's charm. This change of scenery brought a surprising and new element to the morning ride.

Breakfast, once a routine affair, changed in a wonderful way. Aarav drew inspiration from the different flavours of Indian cuisine and experimented with regional dishes and spices. The morning meal became a celebration of culinary diversity, with the aroma of spices wafting through the air, reminiscent of the bustling street stalls.

The work area, previously confined to a specific room, was moved to the balcony overlooking the city. Here, surrounded by the sounds of the waking city, Aarav found a new perspective that enlivened his work. The morning routine blended seamlessly into the vibrant life of Mumbai, transforming mundane tasks into opportunities for creativity.

Mindful moments and acts of kindness extended not only to the house, but also to the neighbours in the bustling residential complex. Inspired by the Indian philosophy 'Vasudhaiva Kutumbakam' (the world is a family), Aarav began to leave positive messages for his neighbours that went beyond the boundaries of routine.

Aarav's playlist, once a mix of familiar tunes, morphed into a melodic journey through the various genres of Indian music. From classical ragas to modern Bollywood beats, every note sounded like a promise of a day filled with the vibrancy of Indian culture.

Amidst the structured routine, Aarav focused on spontaneity in the sense of 'jugaad' – the art of frugal innovation. The script of the day became improvisation, leaving room for unexpected opportunities that seamlessly blended into daily life.

Sport, which used to be a predictable routine, was replaced by the diversity of Indian traditions. Aarav incorporated yoga and traditional dance forms, infusing his mornings with the rhythmic energy of India's cultural heritage. The routine became a celebration of movement and vitality, reflecting the ancient wisdom of Ayurveda.

Nature beckoned, and Aarav responded by greening his balcony. Amidst potted plants and the scent of blooming flowers, the morning routine became a communion with nature, reflecting the close connection many Indian households have with the natural world.

Visual inspiration adorned the walls, reflecting the kaleidoscope of India's artistic heritage. Paintings depicting vibrant landscapes, motivational quotes in different languages and images capturing the essence of festivals adorned Aarav's living space. The morning routine unfolded against a backdrop of visual inspiration; a canvas painted with the colours of India's diversity.

And so, in the heart of Mumbai, Aarav discovered that thinking outside the box is not just a concept, but also a way to capture the rich diversity of Indian life. Every morning became a celebration of culture, tradition and creativity that blended seamlessly into everyday life. Aarav's story also inspired others in the city of dreams to discover the magic that lies in the art of thinking outside the box. And as Aarav shared these new experiences with his family during morning rituals, the warmth and joy of this creative journey became a common tapestry that united all members in a beautiful dance of tradition and innovation.

In the bustling city of Mumbai, where the vibrant tapestry of daily life unfolded, Aarav was not only an explorer in his personal daily life, but also a dedicated manager in a local tech company. Aarav's journey of discovering creativity and breaking out of routine extended to his role as a leader as well.

As Aarav immersed himself in his day-to-day work, he found innovative ways to foster a culture of flexibility and work-life balance in his team. Recognizing the shift in the world of work, Aarav encouraged telecommuting so that his team had the freedom to choose the environment that best suited their productivity. He believed that flexibility was not just an advantage, but a fundamental shift towards a more adaptable and productive workforce.

When solving problems, Aarav approached the challenges with an open mind. The traditional hierarchical structure gave way to collaborative problem-solving sessions where ideas could flow freely. Aarav's commitment to creative thinking went beyond personal routines; it became a cornerstone of his leadership approach and inspired his team to find unconventional solutions.

Communication within the team flourished under Aarav's leadership. He encouraged an open dialog where team members felt comfortable sharing their thoughts and ideas. Aarav's mornings often began with a short virtual meeting that set the tone for the day and fostered a sense of connection between team members, even if they were miles apart.

For Aarav, decision-making was a collective effort. He believed in the power of diverse perspectives and inclusive decision making. By involving team members in the decision-making process, Aarav not only ensured better results but also instilled a sense of ownership in his subordinates.

Aarav knew the importance of continuous learning and personal development, not only for himself but also for his team. He encouraged skill building, provided opportunities for professional development and celebrated the individual achievements of his team members. The culture of learning became a shared journey of personal development.

In the area of relationships, Aarav fostered a supportive and collaborative environment. The camaraderie that developed within the team transcended professional boundaries. Aarav, who was originally a manager, became a mentor and friend who forged strong interpersonal bonds and strengthened the cohesion of the team.

Leisure and hobbies were not neglected in Aarav's management philosophy. He recognized the importance of recreation, introduced wellness initiatives and encouraged his team members to pursue hobbies and interests outside of work. Aarav believed that a well-rounded individual is not only beneficial in the workplace, but also for society as a whole.

When the working day turned into the evening, Aarav made sure that his team members had the freedom to relax and unwind. Flexible working hours and respect for personal time became an integral part of the evening routine, contributing to a healthy work-life balance that promoted wellbeing and overall job satisfaction.

As a manager and leader, Aarav recognized the importance of a good night's rest for optimal performance. He promoted a culture that prioritized rest and recovery, knowing that a well-rested team is more likely to contribute creatively and effectively to the challenges of the next day.

In this dynamic story of Aarav, the manager, his commitment to flexibility, promoting work-life balance and fostering a culture of creativity became important not only to his personal day-to-day, but also to the success and well-being of his team. His leadership style reflected the essence of lateral thinking and created an environment where innovation thrives and every team member feels inspired to give their best.

Contents

CHAPTER ONE

Attitude Elevation for Limitless Living

ATTITUDE AND MINDSET ADJUSTMENTS in our personal lives are noteworthy shifts in the ways we approach, think about and perceive many facets of our life. These alternations may have an impact on our attitudes, actions, and responses to the circumstances.

In the pages of my life story, *Mindset Shift* has become a cherished companion that takes me on a journey deep into the core of my being. It's like the soothing melody you hear on a rainy day — it speaks to your soul. When I turn a page, I think about how I see the world and how I've learned to interpret life's experiences. I came across this wonderful concept of shifting consciousness, and I can tell you it's not just words, it's a story that touched my heart. It's like freeing yourself from old, limiting thoughts and embracing a brighter, more open mindset. It's a journey that feels like a warm hug to my soul.

One part that touched me was this story about transitioning from a fixed mindset to a growth mindset. The words painted a vivid picture — a tiny seed of faith sprouting into a blossoming garden of possibility. I could almost feel the transformative power in those words.

And you know what?

As I read, I nodded in agreement and a thought popped into my head, *what if I could make that kind of change in my own life?* It felt like a light bulb went on and then I remembered a dialog from the book that stuck with me: *Abilities aren't fixed; they're like seeds waiting to be nurtured.*

In the simplicity of these words, I saw a reflection of my journey — letting go of old beliefs, opening up to new possibilities, and finding the courage to nurture the seeds of change. *Mindset Shift* isn't just a book, but my coach, whispering to my heart that growth isn't just about what I achieve, but about the wonderful changes that are taking place within me.

Attitude shift has also become a calming companion to guide me through the emotional landscape of how

I respond to the world around me. It's like having a heart-to-heart conversation with an old friend who knows what makes my emotions tick. I've been thinking about how attitude shapes our experiences. It's not just about what happens, it's about how we feel, think, and react. The concept of attitude —change - changing the mood of our emotional and behavioral responses.

There's a beautiful story that struck me. It's about moving from a negative mindset, where change feels like an unwelcome visitor, to an adaptable and positive mindset that welcomes new opportunities with open arms. True to the motto: *Life, throw everything you've got at me — I'm ready for the dance!*

And then there is this dialog that impressed me: *Accept challenges like stepping stones.* Those words stuck with me and I thought: *What if challenges weren't obstacles, but stepping stones to something better?* That's a powerful thought that feels like a soothing whisper amid life's storms.

As I read on, I nodded in agreement and thought, *yes, I can welcome change like an old friend, find joy in the journey, and face challenges with courage.* It's not just about a new attitude, but a conversation that invites me to reshape my life.

Attitude shift is a personal journey. It's about choosing optimism, resilience, and a proactive mind. It's about turning over a new leaf with a smile and an open heart.

How attitudes and behaviors change:

1. *Self-reflection:*

Self-reflection is the compass that leads people on an inward journey to explore their beliefs, perceptions, and emotional responses. Through self-reflection, you can unravel the layers of your thought patterns and identify areas where change is needed.

Take a new perspective on life and turn ordinary moments into valuable lessons

This rephrased sentence suggests the idea of approaching life with a new or different perspective. In this way, everyday moments that seem ordinary at first glance can be seen as opportunities to learn and gain valuable insights. The emphasis is on the transformative power of looking at life from a different viewpoint and angle the potential for growth and wisdom in everyday experiences. By taking time to reflect, you can understand the roots of your mindset and attitude and pave the way for cognizant change.

Curiosity grows with questioning, and life is enriched

This statement emphasizes that our curiosity naturally grows when we engage with questions. When our curiosity expands, it contributes to a more vibrant and enriched life. When we ask questions and seek knowledge, we not only satisfy our innate curiosity but also expand the depth and quality of our experiences, making our lives more meaningful and fulfilling. In essence, the process of questioning becomes a catalyst for an enriched and purposeful life.

Self-reflection sparks curiosity about our thought processes and fosters a desire for growth and a willingness to challenge existing beliefs.

When we take the time to reflect on our beliefs, values, and reactions, we can identify areas where change could be beneficial. Self-awareness is the first step to change.

2. Learning and Growth:

Learning and growth is the journey in which we acquire new knowledge, new experiences, and new skills that open the door to change. Learning broadens the horizons of our understanding, challenges us, and changes our perspectives.

Continuous personal development is a lifelong focus

conveys the idea that the process of individual growth and self-improvement is something that one pursues consistently throughout one's life. It emphasizes the continuous nature of personal development and suggests that there is always room for learning, advancement, and self-improvement and that this commitment to growth extends to the end of one's life. Every bit of wisdom one gains becomes a catalyst for change and fosters adaptability and resilience. In the realm of mindset, the transition from a rigid mindset to a growth-oriented mindset is fostered by a constant thirst for knowledge.

Age has no bearing on a person's vitality; it is the attitude of learning that truly characterizes old age, be it at twenty or eighty.

The reworded sentence conveys that a person is not considered *"old"* because of their chronological age, but because of their willingness or unwillingness to continue learning. Whether someone is twenty or eighty years old, if they stop learning and acquiring new knowledge, they are considered old in terms of their intellectual and personal development. The emphasis is on the importance of a lifelong commitment to learning and openness to new experiences, regardless of age.

A growth mindset means that you see challenges as opportunities to learn and improve and that learning serves as a vehicle for this transformative journey. With the right mindset, you can respond to the subtleties of life by learning with an open heart.

Participate in an activity every day that takes you out of your comfort zone.

Every step out of your comfort zone is a step towards personal growth and forms an attitude that welcomes change and new opportunities. Exposure to new ideas, experiences, and knowledge can challenge existing beliefs, broaden your perspective, and change your attitude toward continuous learning and personal development.

3. Challenging Limiting Beliefs:

To challenge limiting beliefs, one must courageously explore and question deeply held beliefs that can hinder personal growth and a positive perspective.

Use your mind to heal your life; don't rely on others.

This statement emphasizes the idea that everyone can create healing in their lives. It encourages personal responsibility and independence and suggests not relying solely on external sources or others for personal healing. The core of the message is to recognize the power of one's thoughts, beliefs, and attitudes to promote positive change and well-being. It emphasizes the importance of taking proactive steps and owning the path to healing and personal growth. This introspection allows people to recognize self-imposed limitations and opens the door to a new mindset —that recognizes the potential for change and growth.

How you see yourself and the thoughts you have can determine the course of your life. Choose to think positively and stay away from negativity to find a positive path for your life.

This is the essence of a growth mindset that challenges the fixed idea that *abilities are predetermined*. When you confront limiting attitudes, you must recognize the impact they have on overcoming life's challenges.

By confronting limiting ideas, you may create a mental shift that encourages perseverance, optimism, and taking charge of life's obstacles. By moving from the mindset of "*I can't*" to "*I can*", you can create important opportunities and cultivate a positive outlook.

4. Coping with Challenges:

Overcoming challenges plays a central role in the way to a changed mindset and attitude. In difficult moments, people have the opportunity to test the strength of their beliefs and reactions. Challenges act as crucibles that refine one's character and foster resilience. In overcoming difficulties lies an opportunity for personal growth and the development of a positive attitude.

A proverb puts it in a nutshell,

In the middle of every crisis lies a great opportunity

meaning that while challenges may be scary, they hold the potential for profound positive change. Every obstacle becomes a stepping stone, as the saying goes.

5. Setting and Achieving Goals:

Setting and achieving goals acts like a guiding star that directs our focus and efforts toward a specific goal. When we set *specific, measurable, achievable, relevant, and time-bound (SMART)* goals, we create a roadmap for personal growth.

Pursuing these goals challenges our current mindset and forces us to overcome obstacles and expand our capabilities.

If you don't have goals in your life, you won't achieve anything. It's important to set goals for each phase of your life.

Goals give us direction, motivate us, and reinforce our belief that change is inevitable. Achieving these milestones not only means success but also promotes a positive attitude.

If you have a clear goal in your life and are working hard to achieve it, make sure that you follow the path you take carefully. Avoid taking shortcuts to achieve your life goals.

The above statement explains that, If you're striving for certain goals in your life, you must be clear about the direction you want to take. The path to achieving your goals requires a thoughtful approach that emphasizes the importance of your chosen path. While it may be tempting to look for shortcuts or quick fixes, we advise you to avoid such approaches. Instead, focus on the journey and recognize that the process of achieving your goals is just as important as the goal itself. This guide encourages you to adopt a cautious and deliberate attitude that reminds you to stay true to your values and keep working towards your goals, even when you face challenges or feel the lure of faster paths.

The process of setting and achieving goals becomes a catalyst for a shift in mindset and attitude that encourages a proactive and optimistic view of challenges and opportunities alike. Working towards and achieving goals can bring about positive change. Successes big and small contribute to a more optimistic and proactive attitude.

6. Surrounding Environment:

The environment plays a crucial role in changing mindsets and attitudes, acting as a silent but influential architect of personal change. Like a garden that encourages or hinders the growth of its flowers, our surroundings, with their people, places, and cultural influences, contribute to the development of our perspectives. The world we live in is shaped by our thoughts and the thoughts of future generations. To make the world a better place, we need to keep contributing through creative thinking. A positive and supportive environment can be a catalyst to foster a growth mindset and a positive attitude. Surrounding ourselves with people who inspire and encourage us can have a huge impact. Exposure to different ideas, cultures, and experiences broadens our horizons and challenges entrenched attitudes. The people we interact with, the books we read, and the media we consume can influence our mindset and attitude. It is important to choose a positive and supportive environment.

7. Mindfulness and Presence:

Mindfulness and presence play a central role in the profound shift towards a positive mindset and an adaptive attitude. Mindfulness means fully engaging with the present moment and developing an awareness of thoughts and feelings without judging them. It acts like a gentle anchor that prevents you from dwelling on the past or worrying about the future. Those who practice mindfulness witness the power of the now and realize that the present is where true change happens.

Live in the present moment. Don't dwell on past moments, whether they have brought suffering or happiness, and don't fixate on future moments that could bring happiness. This realization becomes a driving force that enables the shift from a rigid mindset to one that allows for growth and possibility. Mindfulness also promotes resilience and makes it possible to face challenges with greater ease, as Jon Kabat-Zinn says:

You can't stop the waves, but you can learn to surf them.

This resilience is the cornerstone of a positive mindset that sees challenges not as insurmountable obstacles, but as opportunities for growth. With the help of mindfulness and presence, people embark on a transformative journey, enjoying the richness of each moment and developing a story of personal growth. Practicing mindfulness and being present at the moment can shift our mindset from the past or worrying about the future to appreciating the present and embracing change.

8. Cultivating Gratitude:

Cultivating gratitude plays an important role on the path to changing mentalities and attitudes. It acts as a breeding ground that promotes the growth of positivity, resilience, and a deeper appreciation of life. When we consciously cultivate gratitude, we shift our focus from what we lack to what we have, and this has a positive impact on our attitude.

As Melody Beattie said so beautifully,

Gratitude gives meaning to our past, brings peace for today, and creates a vision for tomorrow.

It enables us to find meaning even in challenging moments and changes our attitude towards adversity. Gratitude becomes a powerful broadcaster in the storm of change, guiding us through shifts in our mindset and attitude with a spirit of appreciation and resilience. When we focus on gratitude, we can recognize the positive aspects of our lives and develop a more optimistic and appreciative attitude.

10 creative ways to encourage a change in attitude:

1. *Keep a gratitude journal:* Keep a daily gratitude journal and write down three things you are grateful for. This exercise promotes a positive attitude.

2. *Artwork with affirmations:* Design visual affirmations and create them as artwork. Hang them up in your workspace to reinforce your positive beliefs.

3. *Challenge your comfort zone:* Regularly participate in activities that push you to your limits. This can be anything from public speaking to trying out a new hobby.

4. *Mindful breathing exercises:* Build mindfulness into your daily routine with short breathing exercises. Focus on your breath to clear your mind and promote a calm mindset.

5. *Create a vision board:* Create a vision board with pictures and quotes that represent your goals. Hang it up where you can see it every day to motivate you.

6. *Role reversal:* Imagine you are in another person's shoes, especially in difficult situations. This promotes empathy and a more understanding way of thinking.

7. *Storytelling through music:* Create a playlist that reflects your desired attitude. Use music to change your mood and perspective.

8. *Random acts of kindness:* Do small, unexpected acts of kindness for others. This strengthens your sense of purpose and contributes to a positive attitude.

9. *Mind-altering books:* Read books that challenge your current thinking or give you new perspectives. Look for literature that inspires you to grow and be positive.

10. *Visualization exercises:* Do guided visualizations to imagine yourself achieving your goals. This will help you develop a positive mindset by imagining success.

CHAPTER TWO

The Art of Observation, the Thrill of Exploration

HAVE YOU EVER TAKEN a moment to look around you and see the world unfolding before you? It's more than just seeing; it's an art, a connection to the heartbeat of life. Have you ever wondered what stories are hidden in the everyday moments that make life extraordinary?

Imagine the rustle of leaves, the laughter of a stranger passing by, or the gentle sigh of the evening breeze. Do you sometimes discover the magic in these small, unnoticed details? In these nuances lies the true meaning of observation: we understand the patterns and behaviors that shape our world.

Let's bring this closer to your journey. Have you ever felt the impact that observation has on your decisions? It's not just a passive action, but a guide, a compass that leads you to decisions that align with your heart. Imagine the warmth of self-awareness, those aha moments when you realize how much observation determines your path.

In the web of personal life, observation becomes a trusted friend. Have you ever felt how it deepens your relationships with others? It's a bridge between souls, fostering understanding and empathy. Have you ever experienced the joy of truly seeing and being seen and making connections that go beyond the surface?

In the simplicity of observation, we find a path to wisdom and growth. Have you ever thought about the secrets it holds for resilience and adaptability? As humble observers, can we become the storytellers of our journey?

As we journey through the pages of life, we should appreciate the art of observation. What stories do they hold for you? What feelings do they awaken in the silent chambers of your heart? In the dance of observation, let us find the melody that echoes in our souls.

Think of the moments when a simple observation has led to a profound realization. Have you ever witnessed a sunrise and felt the promise of a new day? Or, while quietly observing a loved one, have you discovered layers of their personality that you hadn't noticed before? These are the threads of the rich tapestry of life that is woven by the simple act of paying attention.

Consider the role observation plays in decision-making. Have you ever found yourself at a crossroads and not known which way to go? In such moments, careful observation becomes a beacon that guides you to a decision that aligns with your deepest values. It's as if the world is giving you a roadmap for your journey with its subtle clues.

Now let's look at the emotional resonance of observation. Imagine a moment of connection with a friend, where a shared glance says more than words ever could. Have you ever felt the power of silent observation, the unspoken understanding that connects people? In moments like these, we realize how important it is to be present and to notice and appreciate the unique beauty of each person.

Think about the role observation plays in fostering empathy. Have you ever put yourself in another person's shoes by observing and listening to them closely? This is a transformative experience that breaks down barriers and builds bridges of understanding. In these cases, observation becomes a tool to create a compassionate and connected world.

Think about how observation evolves throughout life. As we grow, our perspectives change and what we once innocently observed takes on new meaning. Have you ever visited a place from your past and viewed it through the lens of your present self? It's a poignant reminder of the journey we've taken, shaped by the observations that have molded us along the way.

Think of the connection between observation and creativity. Have you ever been inspired by the details of the world around you? Whether it's the play of light on water or the intricate pattern of a flower, observation opens the door to a world of creativity. It's a reminder that beauty lies in the ordinary, waiting to be discovered by those who take the time to observe it.

Now let's explore the symbiotic relationship between observation and resilience. Have you ever faced adversity and drawn strength from the lessons of past experiences? Like a seasoned observer, you walk through challenges with a deeper understanding and utilize the wisdom you've gained from the ebb and flow of life.

On the great tapestry of personal growth, observation is the loom through which we weave the threads of our experiences. Have you ever noticed how the patterns of your life unfold and how you connect the dots between seemingly unrelated events? It's the art of observation that allows us to recognize the story of our journey and discover the chapters of joy, sorrow, and everything in between.

As we move through the complexity of relationships, think about the role observation plays in nurturing relationships. Have you ever had the feeling of being seen by someone who notices the subtleties of your facial expressions and gestures? It's a profound experience where observation becomes a language of love that transcends words and creates bonds that stand the test of time.

Now let's turn to the world outside of us. Have you ever observed nature and marveled at its beauty? Whether it's the dance of the leaves in the wind or the majesty of a mountain peak, nature invites us to observe its wonders closely. In these moments, we become humble witnesses to the magnificence of the universe and find solace and inspiration in the simplicity of observation.

Consider the transformative power of observation to cultivate gratitude. Have you ever taken a moment to appreciate the small pleasures that often go unnoticed? It could be the warmth of sunlight on your face or the laughter of children playing. Observation becomes a gateway to gratitude and allows us to enjoy the richness of life.

Now let's explore the intersection between observation and personal reflection. Have you ever closely observed your thoughts and feelings? It's an inward journey where self-knowledge blossoms through a careful examination of the inner landscape. In these moments of introspection, observation becomes a mirror that reflects the depths of our being.

Reflect on how observation in the ebb and flow of life becomes a compass to guide us through uncertainty. Have you ever faced a challenge and draw strength from the lessons of past experiences? It's as if each observation becomes a stepping stone that paves the way to resilience and growth.

As we close this chapter on observation, think of the lasting invitation it extends. Have you ever embraced the beauty of observing life with an open heart and a curious mind? It's an ongoing journey, a dance with the ever-changing rhythm of existence. In the simplicity of observation, we not only find answers but also a continuous unfolding of the questions that shape our understanding of ourselves and the world around us.

Now let's move into the equally enchanting realm of exploration, where curiosity becomes our compass, guiding us to the undiscovered corners of existence. Have you ever felt the thrill of going beyond the familiar and embracing the unknown with an open heart? Exploration is more than a physical journey; it's a state of mind, an invitation to dance with the possibilities that await us.

Imagine standing on the threshold of a new experience, an unknown territory waiting for you. Have you ever wondered what stories unfold when you venture beyond your comfort zone? When we embark on a journey of discovery, we break through the boundaries of routine and allow the diverse landscapes of life to shape us.

Think about how important exploration is to expanding our horizons. Have you ever marveled at the richness of life that reveals itself to you when you travel, whether to distant lands or the unexplored realms of your community? Exploration is the key that opens the doors to understanding, offering a kaleidoscope of perspectives and a deeper connection to the world.

Have you ever taken the plunge into a new hobby, skill, or passion? Through exploration, we discover hidden facets of ourselves and unleash potential waiting to be discovered. Imagine the joy of self-discovery, where each exploration becomes a brushstroke on the canvas of your evolving identity.

In the intimate dance of personal relationships, consider the role of exploration in fostering connection. Have you ever shared new experiences with a loved one and created memories that have deepened your bond? Exploration becomes a shared journey, a shared adventure that strengthens the ties that bind us.

Think about the emotional resonance of exploration. Have you ever felt a sense of liberation and empowerment when you ventured down unknown paths? In these moments of courageous exploration, we overcome self-imposed boundaries and have the courage to redefine our story.

Remember that we're always breaking new ground in the course of our lives. Have you ever noticed that as we age, the landscape of our interests changes, inviting us to discover new passions and redefine our goals? Exploration becomes a lifelong companion, an ever-present guide that encourages us to seek, discover, and reinvent.

How they complement each other:

Let us now weave together the threads of observation and exploration. Have you ever observed how these two elements dance in harmony, influencing and enriching each other? Imagine the synergy: Observation lays the foundation for exploration, and exploration in turn deepens our ability to differentiate observation.

In the great tapestry of personal and collective growth, observation and exploration are the dynamic duo. Have you ever thought about the influence they have on your path? It is a constant interplay, a dance of awareness and curiosity that drives us forward. In this intricate choreography, we not only find the answers to our questions but also an ever-expanding universe of possibilities waiting to be explored. So let the art of observation and the spirit of inquiry guide us as we discover the profound beauty and infinite potential of the human experience.

10 creative ways to use observation and exploration to foster creativity:

1. *Micro-explorations:* Zoom in on tiny details in your immediate surroundings. Observe the subtleties of objects, textures, or patterns that often go unnoticed.

2. *Sensory observations:* Engage your senses fully. Close your eyes and focus on the sounds, smells, and textures around you. How do these sensory impressions influence your perception?

3. *Journey mapping:* Document your experiences during the day in visual or written form. Create a

map of your day and note interesting encounters or moments that stand out to you.

4. *Immersive experiences:* Immerse yourself in unfamiliar environments or activities. Take part in events, visit places, or try out hobbies outside your comfort zone to gain new perspectives.

5. *Observational walks:* Take deliberate walks in different environments. Pay attention to the people, architecture, and nature around you. Document your observations with sketches, photos, or notes.

6. *Explore through different lenses:* Look at the same topic through different lenses, both figuratively and literally. For example, look at a problem from different perspectives or use different camera filters to capture an object.

7. *Random prompts:* Use random prompts or challenges to guide your observations. Create a list of prompts or draw them from a hat to determine what you want to focus on in your exploration.

8. *Storytelling with objects:* Choose any objects and makeup stories about them. This exercise stimulates the imagination and helps you to see ordinary objects in a new light.

9. *Explore time travel:* Imagine traveling back or forward in time. What would the same place or

scenario look like in a different time? This exercise stimulates your creativity by incorporating historical or futuristic elements into your observations.

10. *Mapping emotions:* Create an emotional map of a place or experience. Observe how your feelings change as you move through different spaces and consider how emotions influence your perception.

CHAPTER THREE

Elevate Your Days, Break Your Ways

ROUTINE BREAKERS GENERALLY REFER to activities or changes that interrupt or break the habitual or established routine. Routines are often necessary for efficiency and stability, but bringing variety and novelty into our lives can have many positive effects.

In our daily lives, interruptions to routine are the living threads that weave moments of magic and meaning. Have you ever paused in the middle of your routine and rejoiced in the unexpected whisper of spontaneity? Imagine that: The familiar melody of your daily symphony is interrupted by the sweet dissonance of a newfound curiosity. Can you feel the subtle shift, like the turn of a page, as routine meets the uncharted territory of possibility?

Think about how beautiful it's to engage with the unwritten scenes of life. What about engaging in cultural exploration in the midst of our busy schedules and savouring the rich diversity of experiences and tastes? Can you taste the unknown, feel the heartbeat of a different rhythm beneath the soles of your feet as you tread unexplored paths?

In this delicate dance between routine and revelation, personal growth takes centre stage. Have you ever marvelled at the kaleidoscope of your own potential that reveals itself when you step outside the boundaries of your routine? Imagine the excitement of learning a new dance, whether it's a physical skill, a mental challenge or an emotional revelation. Can you hear the applause of your inner self when you master a new step, overcome a hurdle or simply enjoy the joy of the unexpected?

But when we set out to break the routine, there is also an undertone of mindfulness. What if we found solace in moments of reflection and gratitude in our search for newness? Can you imagine how nice it would be to take a break, go on a digital detox and allow the symphony of your thoughts to transport you to a state of inner peace?

Perhaps the most poignant notes in this melody are those of connection and compassion. Have you ever ventured beyond the walls of your routine to help someone, share a smile or simply be there for someone else? Imagine the laughter shared, the stories exchanged, the weaving of hearts into a tapestry of common humanity.

Walking the fine line between routine and extraordinary, we should celebrate the milestones and cherish the chapters that unfold between the lines. Can you feel the warmth of gratitude, the gentle pull of inspiration, when we allow the routine breakers to paint the canvas of our lives with the colours of joy, growth and connection?

Here are a few examples and benefits of routine breakers:

Creativity and innovation: doing things differently or trying new activities can foster creativity and innovation. Breaking out of routine allows your mind to discover new perspectives and ideas.

Stress reduction: Routines can become monotonous and lead to stress. Variety can reduce stress by making everyday life more exciting and adventurous.

Personal growth: By stepping out of your comfort zone and trying new things, you can develop personally. This allows you to discover new skills, interests and facets of your personality.

Improved productivity: Interrupting your routine can prevent burnout and increase productivity. Taking short breaks or incorporating different tasks into your day can help maintain focus and prevent fatigue.

Increased well-being: Activities that deviate from your routine can contribute to your overall well-being. They can improve mood, reduce boredom and increase satisfaction with life.

Create memories: Breaks in routine often involve experiences and activities that create lasting memories. These memories can enrich and fill your life.

Examples of routine interruptions include a spontaneous weekend getaway, a new hobby, attending events or gatherings, or simply a change in routine. The most important thing is to incorporate elements of unpredictability and variety into your routine to promote your personal development and a more fulfilling life.

10 creative ways to bring routine into your life:

1. *Random Acts of Kindness Day:* Set aside one day a week to perform random acts of kindness. This can be as simple as buying someone a coffee, leaving an encouraging note, or offering a helping hand. Not only does it loosen up your routine, but it also spreads a positive vibe.

2. *Adventure jar:* Create an adventure jar filled with different activities or challenges. Choose one idea from the jar each day and integrate it into your daily routine. This could be trying out a new recipe, a spontaneous day trip, or learning a new skill.

3. *Theme days:* Dedicate certain days of the week to different themes. For example, have a *"DIY Wednesday"* where you do a creative project or a *"Tech-Free Thursday"* where you switch off and focus on analogy activities.

4. *Reverse routine day:* Add variety to your daily routine by doing tasks in reverse order. If you normally start your day with breakfast, try having dinner in the morning. This unconventional approach can give your habits a new perspective.

5. *Quiet retreat hours:* Take a few hours a week as quiet retreat time. Turn off your electronic devices, create a quiet space, and use this time for reflection, meditation, or calming activities to disconnect from the noise of everyday life.

6. *Wildcard lunch:* Designate one day as your *"wildcard lunch"* day. Instead of your usual meal, choose a dish you've never tried before or let someone else choose for you. This creates an element of surprise and introduces you to new flavors.

7. *Switch to commuter mode:* If possible, change up your commute routine. Walk or bike instead of driving, take public transportation or carpool. Changing your mode of transportation not only changes your routine but can also give you a new perspective on your surroundings.

8. *Unplanned day off:* From time to time, declare a *"day off"* where you have no activities planned. Let the day be spontaneous and leave room for spontaneous adventures, whether it's exploring a new area or simply enjoying a day of leisure.

9. *Digital detox hours:* Take a few hours each week for a digital detox. Turn off your phone, computer, and other screens and use this time for analogy activities like reading a book, drawing, or enjoying nature.

10. *Themed dress-up days:* Introduce themed dress-up days into your daily routine. Whether it's *"Throwback Thursday"* with retro outfits *or "Fantasy Friday"* where you dress up as your favorite character - bring a playful and creative element to your daily attire.

CHAPTER FOUR

Connect the Dots of Knowledge

INTERDISCIPLINARY THINKING IS THE ability to integrate and apply knowledge, concepts, and approaches from different disciplines or fields of study. In our lives, interdisciplinary thinking means looking beyond the boundaries of a single discipline and using insights and methods from different sources to solve problems, make decisions, and manage different aspects of life.

Think of your life as a living mosaic, where different pieces of knowledge and experience come together to create a beautiful blend. It's like mixing the colors of psychology with the patterns of business and the tones of science with the wisdom of philosophy. Imagine what could happen if we explored beyond our usual areas of interest. Could the answers to our big questions be found by bringing together ideas from different fields? How might this blend of thought and insight illuminate the uncertain areas of our lives?

As we grow personally, being open to different perspectives is like a guide to help us learn more and be more creative. Imagine the moment when different pieces of information come together and generate new ideas. What if combining thoughts that have nothing to do with each other can make ordinary things extraordinary? Could this kind of thinking help us discover new things about ourselves?

In our daily interactions, the ability to talk about different topics is like building bridges between people with different experiences. Imagine how powerful it can be when people from different backgrounds come together and share their knowledge. What if our ability to collaborate across different fields helped us understand each other better? Can this kind of thinking create connections that touch our hearts?

When it comes to making decisions, a mix of perspectives is like a compass that guides us through uncertainty. Imagine a situation where different perspectives influence the decisions we make. What if looking at things from different angles could make our decisions smarter? Could combining insights from different areas help us make better decisions?

In the world of creativity, thinking in different areas is like a delicate flower blooming in a garden full of ideas. Imagine how unique and exciting it could be when ideas from different fields come together. What if the combination of creativity from different areas could make something extraordinary out of the ordinary? Can this blend of creative thinking appeal to our deepest emotions?

In the face of change, the ability to adapt with different skills and insights is like a reliable guidepost. Imagine the strength that comes when we draw from a variety of skills. What if being open to the unexpected is the key to dealing with life's ups and downs? Could this diverse thinking be like a protective cloak that helps us face the uncertainties of life with grace?

Let's look at the idea of interdisciplinary thinking in our history as something powerful, as a light that illuminates the potential in all of us. Within this blend of knowledge and collaborative thinking might be a story that speaks to the core of what makes us human — a story that transcends categories and creates connections that resonate deeply within us.

Here are a few ways interdisciplinary thinking can show up in your personal life:

Problem-solving: when you face challenges or complex situations, people with interdisciplinary thinking skills can use knowledge and ideas from different fields to come up with creative and effective solutions. They can consider perspectives from psychology, business, science, and other fields to solve a particular problem.

Innovation: Interdisciplinary thinking promotes innovation by combining ideas and approaches from different areas. This can lead to the development of new products, services, or approaches that might not have been recognized within the confines of a single discipline.

Learning and growth: Incorporating interdisciplinary thinking into personal development allows individuals to continuously learn and grow. By exploring different areas of knowledge, people can gain a broader understanding of the world and improve their adaptability and resilience.

Communication and collaboration: People who can think across disciplines often find it easier to communicate and collaborate with people from different backgrounds. This is especially valuable in today's interconnected world where collaboration between different disciplines is becoming more common.

Decision-making: Thinking across disciplines can contribute to better decision-making by considering a broader range of factors and perspectives. This can lead to more informed decisions in personal and professional life.

Creativity: The ability to combine ideas from different disciplines is a key element of creativity. Those who think across disciplines are more likely to come up with original and imaginative solutions, whether in art, problem-solving, or everyday tasks.

Adaptability: In a rapidly changing world, the ability to adapt to new situations and challenges is crucial. Interdisciplinary thinking makes individuals more adaptable as they can draw on a variety of skills and knowledge.

To develop interdisciplinary thinking in your personal life, you should explore areas outside your comfort zone, participate in activities that require different skills and be open to learning from different disciplines.

10 creative ways to encourage interdisciplinary thinking:

1. *Book Swap Challenge:* Swap books with someone from a completely different field. Read and collect ideas that you can apply to your field.

2. *Industry Mashup Workshops:* Host workshops that bring together professionals from different industries to solve challenges. Encourage different perspectives to tackle problems.

3. *Creative Analogies:* Create analogies between concepts from your field and other fields. This can lead to new insights and solutions.

4. *Subject-specific techniques in non-subject areas:* Apply techniques that are common in one field to solve problems in another field. For example, you can apply design thinking in corporate strategy.

5. *Interdisciplinary project teams:* Form teams with members from different specialist areas to work on a project. This promotes the exchange of ideas and approaches.

6. *Interdisciplinary conferences:* Attend conferences outside your field to learn about other perspectives and ideas. Look for connections between your field and others.

7. *Explore science fiction:* Read works of science fiction and explore how the technologies and concepts portrayed can be applied or adapted to real-world scenarios.

8. *Cross-disciplinary brainstorming:* During brainstorming sessions, be intentional about bringing

in ideas from other fields. Encourage participants to make connections between seemingly disparate concepts.

9. *Learn new skills:* Acquire skills from a field unrelated to your own. Apply these new skills to your work to bring in new perspectives.

10. *Interdisciplinary networking events:* Attend networking events that bring together professionals from different fields. Take part in discussions to understand challenges and solutions in different industries.

CHAPTER FIVE

Thoughts Unveiled, Creativity Revealed

VISUAL THINKING IS A cognitive process in which visual elements such as pictures, diagrams, tables and other visual aids are used to organize, understand and convey information.

In the stories we write about our lives, visual thinking is like a helpful guide that makes everything clearer. Think of it like a magic paintbrush that transforms our complicated thoughts into simple images. Have you ever noticed how images, like stars in the night sky, can illuminate our ideas?

Let's explore this idea of visual thinking together. Think about your dreams and goals - they're like pieces of a puzzle, and a vision board is like putting those pieces together to create a beautiful picture of what you want. Can you feel your goals becoming more real when you see them visually, like a painting that speaks to your heart? When we learn new things, pictures and images can be very helpful. Imagine flashcards with colourful pictures that make learning fun. Can you imagine that these pictures help you to memorize things better?

Visual thinking also helps us to communicate our feelings. Imagine a powerful image – it can sometimes say more than words. Have you ever felt a strong emotion just because you saw a strong image? When you think of us in quiet moments, imagine a diary with your thoughts and feelings written on the pages like drawings. Can you feel how beneficial it's to express yourself through simple sketches?

Making decisions is easier when we can see our options. Imagine a tree with different branches – each decision is like a leaf on a branch. Can you see how visual thinking makes decisions clearer? And when we plan something, such as a personal project, imagine drawing your ideas on paper. Can you feel the excitement as your plans turn into reality, like a picture coming to life? Visual thinking is like a special language that speaks to our hearts. Can you hear the gentle message that invites you to use your imagination wonderfully?

Visual thinking can play an important role in various aspects of our personal lives:

Problem-solving: visual thinking helps to break down complex problems into visual components, making it easier to analyze them and find solutions. Mind maps, flowcharts, and diagrams can be powerful tools for organizing thoughts and identifying connections.

Set goals: Visual representations of your goals can increase your motivation and clarity. On vision boards, for example, you can put together images and words that represent your wishes and constantly remind you of your goals.

Learning and memorizing: Visual aids can improve learning and retention. Visual summaries and flashcards with pictures or diagrams can make it easier to understand and memorize information.

Creativity: Visual thinking is closely linked to creativity. The use of visual aids can stimulate creative thinking and allow you to explore ideas, connections, and alternatives more freely.

Communication: Visual aids can improve communication by conveying information clearly and concisely. This is particularly useful in personal relationships where visual aids can help express complex feelings or ideas.

Planning and organization: Visual aids such as calendars, charts, and timelines are effective for planning and organizing personal activities. They provide a visual overview of tasks, events, and deadlines.

Reflection and mindfulness: Visual thinking can be a tool for self-reflection. Journaling, sketching, or visual representations of your thoughts and feelings can be therapeutic and promote your personal growth.

Decision making: Visualizing options and consequences can help with decision-making processes. Creating lists of pros and cons, decision trees, or visual matrices can clarify decisions and their possible consequences.

Improving memory: Linking information to visual cues can improve memory. Creating pictures or diagrams of the information you want to remember can help you remember it better.

Personal projects: Whether you're planning a DIY project, organizing an event, or pursuing a hobby, visual thinking can help you sketch out your ideas and track progress.

Visual thinking is a versatile tool that you can use to improve different aspects of your life. It harnesses the power of visual representation to simplify, clarify, and enrich the way we think and interact with the world around us.

10 creative ways to incorporate visual thinking into your creative process:

1. *Mind Mapping:* Create mind maps to visually organize ideas, concepts, and relationships. Use colors, images, and keywords to make connections.

2. *Sketch noting:* Take visual notes by combining drawings, symbols, and text. This method helps to summarize information creatively and memorably.

3. *Storyboarding:* Develop storyboards for projects or ideas. Use a sequence of images to outline the flow and development, especially useful for storytelling and project planning.

4. *Visual analogies:* Represent complex ideas or concepts through visual analogies. Compare abstract concepts with concrete images to improve understanding.

5. *Concept Mapping:* Create visual representations of related concepts and ideas. This method is great for exploring the relationships between different elements.

6. *Create a collage:* Use the technique of collage to express ideas visually. Cut out pictures and words

from magazines or make digital collages to creatively represent your thoughts.

7. *Iconography:* Develop a series of icons or symbols that represent important concepts. This visual shorthand can be a quick and effective way to convey information.

8. *Flowcharts and diagrams:* Design flowcharts and diagrams to visualize processes or systems. Visualizing steps and connections can lead to insights and improvements.

9. *Visual reflection:* Reflect on experiences or ideas in visual journals or diaries. Use drawings, pictures, and symbols to capture feelings and thoughts.

10. *Interactive whiteboarding:* Use digital whiteboards or interactive tools for collaborative visual thinking. This enables real-time participation and dynamic visual design.

CHAPTER SIX

Synergy in Ideas, Beauty in Collaboration

COLLABORATIVE CREATIVITY IN PERSONAL life refers to the process of brainstorming, problem-solving, or creating something new through the joint efforts of several people. It involves combining the unique perspectives, skills, and insights of different people to produce an outcome that is richer, more diverse, and often more innovative than what a single person could achieve alone.

On the pages of the Book of Life, the dance of collaborative creativity unfolds like a tapestry woven from the threads of shared dreams and interwoven goals. Imagine a canvas on which the brushstrokes of several people converge, each stroke reflecting the brilliance of the individual and blending seamlessly into a collective masterpiece. Isn't it fascinating how the symphony of ideas, like musical notes, transforms the mundane into something extraordinary as we traverse the chapters of our journey?

But what is the magic ingredient that transforms a simple meeting into a moment of shared brilliance? Could it be the whispered secrets of brainstorming sessions, where ideas soar to new heights unhindered by the limitations of a solitary mind? One might ask: can the collective heartbeat of a group generate a rhythm that is in tune with the soul of creativity?

Think of the pages turned at family and friend gatherings, where laughter and warmth become ink that writes stories of camaraderie. How does planning an event together become a memory that stands the test of time? Is it the different colors of opinions that paint a richer picture and make the canvas of life more vivid and captivating?

Imagine a communal kitchen where different hands stir the pot, each bringing a pinch of uniqueness to the evening's shared recipe. Does the mingling of flavors symbolize the harmonious fusion of individual tastes into a feast of togetherness?

In the quiet corners of shared problem-solving, where minds sit together and search for solutions, does a mosaic of insights emerge to illuminate the way forward? Can the collective strength of shared burdens forge a bond that withstands the tests of time and adversity?

What if we saw creative hobbies not just as individual pursuits, but as communal expressions of art? Could the echo of a shared passion enhance the beauty of a melody or a brushstroke?

And can the echo of a common goal become the heartbeat of a compassionate society when hands unite for a greater cause? Can the tapestry of collaboration weave a fabric that wraps us all in the warmth of connectedness?

Through these considerations, the narrative unfolds not only as a story but also as an invitation to explore, contribute, and discover the beauty that emerges when hearts and minds unite. So, dear reader, as you navigate the chapters of your own story, consider the magic that unfolds when we embrace the art of collaborative creativity — where the simplest words and gestures, when woven together, create a masterpiece that echoes in the hearts of all who participate in its creation.

In personal contexts, collaborative creativity can manifest itself in different ways:

1. ***Brainstorming with others:*** When you are faced with a personal challenge or creative

project, involving others in a brainstorming session can lead to a wider range of ideas and solutions.

2. ***Teamwork on projects:*** Working together on personal projects such as DIY, artistic endeavors or hobbies allows everyone to contribute their strengths and learn from each other.

3. ***Family or friend get-togethers:*** Planning events or activities with family and friends often requires a collaborative effort, from deciding on the theme of the event to organizing logistics and activities.

4. ***Solving problems together:*** When you are faced with personal problems or need to make important decisions, involving others can give you different perspectives and insights that contribute to more effective problem-solving.

5. ***Creative hobbies with others:*** Sharing creative hobbies such as music, art, or writing with others can lead to unique and inspiring works.

6. ***Community involvement:*** Participation in community projects or volunteer work often requires collaboration and fosters a sense of shared purpose and success.

Collaborative creativity in personal life is not just about achieving a specific outcome, but also about building stronger connections, fostering communication, and creating a supportive environment. It's about recognizing that the collective intelligence and creativity of a group can lead to more diverse, innovative, and fulfilling experiences.

10 creative ways to foster collaborative creativity:

1. ***Brainstorming sessions:***

- Encourage open and unbiased brainstorming in a group.

- Use techniques such as mind mapping or word association to identify connections.

2. ***Visual collaboration boards:***

- Set up a physical or digital board where team members can post visual inspirations, sketches, and ideas.

- Encourage collaboration by allowing individual members to build on each other's images.

3. ***Interactive workshops:***

- Conduct hands-on workshops that require collaboration to solve creative challenges.

- Build-in activities that encourage teamwork and idea sharing.

4. ***Cross-functional teams:***

- Form teams with members from different backgrounds, skills, and expertise.

- Utilize each team member's unique strengths for more comprehensive solutions.

5. ***Online collaboration tools:***

- Utilize digital collaboration platforms that allow team members to work together from different locations in real-time.

- Use tools that facilitate idea sharing, document collaboration, and virtual brainstorming.

6. ***Role reversal exercises:***

- Have team members swap roles to create new perspectives.

- This allows them to look at challenges from different angles, which encourages creative thinking.

7. ***Idea relay:***

- Start with one person proposing an idea and let each team member build on it.

- This iterative process can lead to unexpected and innovative solutions.

8. *Storytelling workshops:*

- Develop a shared story that each team member contributes to.

- This can stimulate creative thinking and promote a shared story.

9. *Visual Thinking Walls:*

- Set up a space where team members can sketch their ideas and share visual representations.

- This fosters a creative atmosphere and allows for easy visualization of concepts.

10. *Feedback and iteration sessions:*

- Conduct regular feedback sessions where team members provide constructive input on each other's ideas.

- Use this feedback loop to iteratively improve and refine creative solutions.

CHAPTER SEVEN

Rethink, Reshape, Revitalize

CHALLENGING CONVENTIONS MEANS QUESTIONING established norms, traditions, or generally accepted beliefs in various areas of life. This concept encourages people to think critically, explore new ideas, and consider alternative perspectives rather than blindly adhering to societal expectations or norms.

Think of your life as a book where you can question the usual ways of doing things. What if we take a closer look at what we believe and ask ourselves if it fits who we are? Can we be brave enough to try new ways of doing things, even if they aren't the usual ones? Think about the expectations that society has of us — do they match what we want for ourselves?

Think of your dreams as a colorful painting. Can we break with what is considered normal and add some bold and different colors? What if we measured our success by how happy we are and not by what everyone else thinks?

Can we let go of the roles that are expected of us when it comes to relationships? Is it possible to build relationships that are true to who we are and not just what is expected of us?

Life is full of change, and that's a good thing. Can we see the beauty in not knowing everything? What if the unexpected parts of life become the most interesting chapters of our story?

So, let's look at our lives like a big adventure book. We can explore who we really are, try new things and not worry too much about what everyone else thinks. That way we can find a way of living that feels right for us. It's like writing our own story — one that stays in our hearts and in the hearts of those who truly understand us.

In our personal lives, challenging conventions can manifest themselves in different ways:

Personal beliefs and values:

This is about examining your own beliefs and values, questioning whether they align with your true self, and being open to re-evaluating and evolving them.

Lifestyle choices:

This may mean questioning conventional lifestyles, such as your job, relationships, or way of life. This may mean choosing a non-traditional career, seeking alternative relationship structures, or opting for an unconventional lifestyle.

Social and cultural expectations:

Challenging conventions can mean challenging societal expectations around gender roles, cultural norms, and other social constructs. This includes breaking away from stereotypes and expectations that may not align with your preferences and desires.

Learning and education:

It encourages a proactive approach to learning and education by challenging traditional educational methods and exploring alternative ways of acquiring knowledge and skills.

Creativity and innovation:

Challenging convention often goes hand in hand with encouraging creativity and innovation. It is about thinking outside the box, exploring new ideas, and pushing the boundaries of what is considered normal or accepted.

Willingness to take risks:

Challenging convention can mean taking risks and stepping out of your comfort zone. This can mean taking unconventional career paths, starting a business, or participating in activities that deviate from societal expectations.

By challenging conventions in our personal lives, we have the opportunity to learn more about ourselves, develop personally, and contribute to positive change. It is about developing curiosity, openness, and a willingness to explore possibilities beyond the status quo.

Creative ways to challenge convention and encourage creativity:

1. Reverse thinking: Approach problems or ideas by looking at the opposite of the norm. This can lead to innovative solutions and new perspectives.

2. Random word association: Connect words that have nothing to do with each other and gather ideas based on these unexpected associations. This technique can break traditional thought patterns.

3. Role reversal: Encourage participants to slip into a different role than the one they are used to. This exercise can lead to unique insights and challenge preconceived notions.

4. Storyboarding: Use visual storytelling techniques such as creating a storyboard to sketch out ideas. This is a great way to analyze complex problems and approach challenges differently.

5. Analogies and metaphors: Describe a problem or concept using analogies or metaphors from unrelated fields. This approach can lead to creative solutions by finding commonalities in different areas.

6. Crowdsourced Solutions: Get input from a group of people outside the team or industry. External perspectives can bring unconventional ideas and challenge established norms.

7. Constraints as catalysts: Embrace constraints and limitations as opportunities for creativity. Artificial constraints can generate innovative solutions to problems.

8. Mind mapping: Create visual mind maps to discover connections between seemingly unrelated concepts. This technique helps to uncover hidden connections and develop unconventional ideas.

9. Parallel thinking: Explore multiple perspectives simultaneously using Edward de Bono's six thinking hats method. This structured approach promotes a more comprehensive view of a problem.

10. Cultural fusion: Fuse elements from different cultures or traditions to create something new. This approach encourages diversity and can lead to the development of unique and innovative solutions.

CHAPTER EIGHT

Overcome, Thrive, Excel

OVERCOMING BLOCKS AND FRUSTRATIONS in our personal lives refers to the ability to overcome obstacles, challenges, or setbacks that may hinder our progress, well-being, or personal development. These blocks and frustrations can manifest in various forms, such as mental barriers, emotional challenges, external circumstances, or a combination of factors.

Life is like a storybook, and sometimes it presents us with great challenges. Imagine a journey with many problems, such as self-doubt, external pressures, and unexpected difficulties. How can we deal with all these difficult times and emerge stronger? We need to ask ourselves: What can we learn from these problems? What good things might be hidden in difficult times? These questions help us to better understand our experiences.

Think of resilience as a special strength that we all have. It's like a strong thread that holds our story together. It quietly says: "*You can do this.*" Imagine a mixture of feelings, like a song being played. When things get tough, emotional intelligence comes into play. Can we handle our feelings well? Can we turn frustration into an opportunity to learn about ourselves?

Life is a bit like a jigsaw puzzle. Challenges are like pieces scattered everywhere. The ability to solve problems helps us to put these pieces together. Can we break big problems into smaller ones? When we find a solution, we see a picture of success.

On this journey, support is like a good friend by our side. Who helps us when things are difficult? It could be a friend, family, or someone we look up to. Asking for help isn't a sign of weakness. It shows that we feel connected to others.

In our life story, it's important to set achievable goals. Every goal is like a sign of progress. Are our goals realistic, or are they too difficult to achieve? Celebrating successes, even small ones, is like marking the good parts of our journey. Do we take a moment to appreciate our successes?

This story is about facing challenges to grow. Like a flower that opens, we grow by learning and adapting to change. Can we accept the ups and downs of life and be willing to change with each new chapter?

We hope that readers who live through this story will find comfort in the simple words. The language speaks to everyone's heart and invites them to think about, feel, and connect with the beautiful and sometimes difficult parts of life. Each word is like a stroke in a painting that paints a clear picture of the human experience.

Here are some important aspects of overcoming blocks and frustrations in your personal life:

1. *Recognize blocks:* The first step is to recognize and understand the obstacles or blocks that are hindering your progress. These can be internal, such as self-doubt or limiting beliefs, or external, such as challenging life circumstances.

2. *Develop resilience:* Resilience is the ability to bounce back from setbacks. It's about cultivating an attitude that sees challenges as opportunities for growth rather than insurmountable obstacles. Resilient people can adapt to adversity and keep moving forward.

3. *Problem-solving skills:* When you develop effective problem-solving skills, you can approach challenges with a strategic mindset. This includes breaking down

complex problems into smaller, more manageable tasks and finding practical solutions.

4. *Emotion regulation:* Managing emotions is crucial when you're faced with obstacles. Emotional intelligence helps you to deal better with frustration, disappointment, and stress. This includes self-awareness, self-regulation, and empathy.

5. *Set yourself realistic goals:* Setting achievable and realistic goals will help you find a clear path. Unrealistic expectations can lead to frustration, so it's important that you set goals that are challenging but achievable.

6. *Seek support:* Don't be afraid to ask friends, family, or professionals for support. Sometimes talking to others about challenges can provide valuable insights, alternative perspectives, and emotional support.

7. *Continuous learning:* Adopt a growth mindset that emphasizes continuous learning and improvement. See challenges as an opportunity to acquire new skills, gain experience, and develop personally.

8. *Adapt to change:* Life is dynamic and situations can change unexpectedly. If you're adaptable, you can change your plans and strategies when necessary. Flexibility is a valuable skill for overcoming unexpected obstacles.

9. *Self-reflection:* When you regularly reflect on your experiences and challenges, you gain insight into patterns of behavior and thinking that can contribute to blockages. This self-awareness is important for your personal growth.

10. *Celebrate successes:* Recognize and celebrate your successes, no matter how small they may be. Recognizing progress boosts self-confidence and motivation and makes it easier to overcome future challenges.

Overcoming blocks and frustrations is an ongoing process that requires self-awareness, resilience and a proactive approach to personal growth. It's about developing the skills and mindset you need to overcome challenges and move forward on your life path.

10 creative ways to overcome creative blocks:

1. *Mindful pauses:* Take short mindfulness or meditation breaks to clear your head. Focus on the present moment to reduce stress and open up new perspectives.

2. *Random word associations:* Make a list of random words and try to associate them with your creative challenge. This can trigger unexpected ideas and associations.

3. *Creative constraints:* Put artificial constraints or limits on your project. Sometimes constraints can stimulate creativity because they force you to think outside the usual parameters.

4. *Reverse thinking:* Consider the opposite of your current ideas or assumptions. This technique often leads to innovative solutions and helps to break out of thinking errors.

5. *Role reversal:* Imagine how someone unrelated to your area of expertise or project would approach the problem. This new perspective can lead to new ideas.

6. *Visual brainstorming:* Use visual aids such as sketches, mind maps, or diagrams to develop ideas. Sometimes visualizing your thoughts can help overcome thinking blocks.

7. *Solve problems together:* Get advice from others. Discuss your challenges with colleagues, friends, or mentors to gain new insights and perspectives.

8. *Retreat to nature:* Take some time out and spend time in nature. Nature has a rejuvenating effect and can provide a mental reset that allows for a more creative mindset.

9. *Creative stimuli:* Use thought-provoking prompts or challenges to guide your thinking. Online resources or

creative prompt cards can serve as a starting point for your ideas.

10. *Thematic exploration:* Delve into an area or topic that is completely foreign to you. Take concepts or ideas from this exploration and see if they can be creatively applied to your original task.

CHAPTER NINE

Where Innovation Sparks Triumph

T HE USE OF TECHNOLOGY in our personal lives means that we use technological tools, devices, and systems to enhance various aspects of our daily activities, communication, and general wellbeing. This can mean integrating technology into different areas of our lives to make tasks more efficient, convenient, and enjoyable.

Technology has played a huge role in the history of our lives, making things easier and connecting us in special ways. Think of our phones – they're like little magic wands that allow us to talk to people no matter how far away they are. But here's a thought: in this world of online information, do we ever stop and ask ourselves what we want to learn or know?

Technology helps us get things done, like a faithful helper guiding us through our daily tasks. But in the midst of all this, do we ever think about what's important to us? With all the entertaining things we find online, like movies and games, don't we sometimes miss out on real relationships with the people around us? We track our steps and our health with cool gadgets, but do we ever look at how our hearts and feelings are doing?

Our homes are getting smarter and smarter, with gadgets that do all sorts of things for us. But do we still have room for the simple, personal moments that make a house a home? There is so much to learn in online courses, but are we learning things that touch our hearts and change us? In the world of online money, do we remember to value the people and shared experiences that matter most?

As we use technology to move around and explore, do we ever stop and ask ourselves about the unexplored parts of ourselves? On social media, where everyone is on their best behavior, do we see past the pictures and the real stories? Do we peel back the layers of technology and reflect on the simple things? In this world of wires and screens, it's our hearts that yearn for real connections and our souls that search for meaning beyond the digital world.

Here are some ways people are using technology in their personal lives:

1. *Communication:* technology facilitates instant communication through various channels such as smartphones, social media, emails, and messaging apps. This allows people to stay in touch with friends, family members, and colleagues even when they aren't around.

2. *Access to information:* The internet provides a huge amount of information that we can access at any time. People use technology to access news, research, educational resources, and other important information to stay informed and make better decisions.

3. *Productivity:* Personal productivity can be significantly increased through the use of technology. Applications and tools such as calendars, task management apps, and collaboration platforms help people organize their schedules, set goals, and complete their tasks more effectively.

4. *Entertainment:* Technology plays a crucial role in entertainment, providing various platforms for streaming music, movies, TV shows, and video games. Virtual reality (VR) and augmented reality (AR) also contribute to immersive entertainment experiences.

5. *Health and fitness:* Wearables and health apps use technology to monitor physical activity, track health metrics, and provide personalized insights. This helps people achieve their fitness goals, monitor their well-being, and make healthier lifestyle choices.

6. *Smart home appliances:* Home automation and smart appliances allow people to control and manage their homes remotely. These include smart thermostats, lighting systems, security cameras, and voice-controlled assistants that increase comfort and energy efficiency.

7. *Learning and skills development:* Online courses, e-learning platforms, and educational apps use technology to provide opportunities for continuous learning and skills development. Individuals can access a wide range of courses and resources to improve their knowledge and skills.

8. *Financial management:* Online banking, budgeting apps, and investment platforms use technology to simplify financial management. People can monitor their accounts, track spending, and make transactions from the convenience of their devices.

9. *Travel and navigation:* GPS navigation, travel apps, and online booking platforms use technology to make travel planning and navigation more efficient. With the

help of technology, people can easily find directions, book accommodation, and explore new places.

10. *Social connections:* Social media platforms allow people to connect with others, share experiences, and build communities. These platforms use technology to create virtual spaces for social interaction and networking.

10 creative ways to use technology to foster creativity:

1. *Digital platforms for collaboration:* Use tools like Slack, Microsoft Teams, or collaborative Google Docs for brainstorming and sharing ideas in real-time among team members.

2. *Virtual reality (VR) for creativity workshops:* Use virtual reality platforms to run immersive and interactive creativity workshops where participants can visualize their ideas in a 3D space.

3. *Online tools for design thinking:* Use design thinking platforms such as Miro or MURAL to facilitate virtual brainstorming sessions, idea mapping, and collaborative problem-solving.

4. *Digital sketching and drawing apps:* Experiment with digital sketching and drawing programs like Procreate or Adobe Fresco to easily create and revise visual concepts.

5. *Augmented reality (AR) for prototyping:* Use augmented reality to create interactive prototypes that allow users to experience product or design concepts in the real world and provide feedback.

6. *Interactive whiteboard apps:* Use interactive whiteboard apps like Explain Everything or Jam board for dynamic and visually engaging presentations that encourage creativity in the classroom or workplace.

7. *AI-powered ideation tools:* Use AI-powered tools like OpenAI's GPT-3 or IBM Watson to come up with creative ideas or unique content and get a fresh perspective on different topics.

8. *Digital music production software:* Use digital audio workstations (DAWs) such as Ableton Live or GarageBand to compose, remix, and experiment with music, opening up new possibilities for musical creativity.

9. *Online coding and programming competitions:* Participate in coding competitions on platforms like Code Pen, Hacker Rank, or GitHub to improve your problem-solving skills and encourage creative coding solutions.

10. *Social media to share ideas:* Use social media platforms to create and share creative content, network with like-minded people, and get feedback

on your work. Platforms such as Instagram, Pinterest, and TikTok can serve as a creative outlet.

CHAPTER TEN

Nurturing Nature, Shaping Tomorrow

ENVIRONMENTAL INFLUENCES IN OUR personal lives refer to the various external factors and conditions that affect a person's development, behavior, and overall well-being. These influences can come from the physical, social, cultural, economic, and ecological aspects of the environment in which a person lives.

Think of your life story as a book in which each chapter is shaped by the world around you. Think of the air you breathe, the sun on your face, and the quiet beauty of nature. They're like the paint on the canvas of your life. How do your background, the people you know, and the community you belong to contribute to the color of your life? Your story also includes the money you have, the opportunities you get, and the challenges you face. How do your school experiences and the way you use technology fit into your story? Can you envision the government and nature as part of your journey?

As you read through the pages of your life, pay attention to the simple but powerful moments — the joy of a sunset, the shared laughter with friends, and the footsteps that echo in time. In this exploration, you'll discover the unique beauty of your story and find connections to the stories of others. Life is like a book, and you're the one turning the pages.

Here are some important aspects of the environmental influences on your personal life:

1. *Physical environment:* the physical environment, such as the quality of air, water, and availability of resources, can have a significant impact on a person's health and lifestyle. For example, living in a polluted area can hurt respiratory health.

2. *Social environment:* The people around us, including family, friends, peers, and community members, contribute to our social environment. Social interactions, relationships, and support systems play a critical role in shaping our beliefs, values, and behaviors.

3. *Cultural environment:* Cultural norms, traditions, and societal expectations influence our personal choices and behaviors. Cultural values can shape our views on education, occupations, relationships, and other aspects of life.

4. *Economic environment:* The economic conditions of the environment, such as employment opportunities, income levels, and economic stability, can influence an individual's access to resources, quality of life, and overall well-being.

5. *Educational environment:* The availability and quality of educational opportunities can affect a person's knowledge, skills, and prospects. Access to education and the learning environment contribute significantly to personal development.

6. *Technological environment:* Advances in technology can affect the way we communicate, work, and access information. The use of technology can affect our daily lives, our relationships, and our overall lifestyle.

7. *Political environment:* Government policies, regulations, and the political climate in a region can affect individuals in different ways. Political stability, legal frameworks, and governance can affect personal freedom, security, and access to resources.

8. *Natural environment:* The state of the natural world, including ecosystems, climate, and biodiversity, can

affect our daily lives. Environmental factors such as climate change, natural disasters, and ecological changes can affect where and how we live.

Understanding and dealing with these environmental influences are important for personal development and well-being. People can adapt to their environment, resist it, or try to change it so that it aligns with their values and goals. Furthermore, recognizing that personal life is connected to the environment in general is crucial for overcoming challenges and promoting a sustainable, healthy lifestyle.

10 creative ways to incorporate environmental influences to foster creativity:

1. *Natural elements in the workspace:* Incorporate natural elements such as plants, natural light, or even a small indoor fountain into your workspace to create a calming and inspiring atmosphere.

2. *Outdoor work sessions:* Take your work or creative activities outdoors. Find a quiet park or garden where you can connect with nature while brainstorming or working on projects.

3. *A color palette inspired by nature:* Choose a color scheme for your workspace or creative projects that

is inspired by nature. Greens, blues, and earthy tones can evoke a sense of calm and creativity.

4. *Walking meetings:* Instead of sitting in a meeting room, take your meetings outside on a walk. The change of environment can generate new ideas and encourage open conversations.

5. *Soundscape of nature:* Create a playlist of nature sounds such as running water, birdsong, or rustling leaves. Play it quietly in the background to encourage concentration and creativity.

6. *Outdoor artistic retreat:* Set up an outdoor creative retreat with comfortable seating, art supplies, and an inspiring view. Use this space for drawing, writing, or brainstorming.

7. *Art installations inspired by nature:* Incorporate nature-inspired art installations or sculptures into your workspace. These can serve as visual stimuli and conversation starters.

8. *Mindful walks in nature:* Take short breaks for mindful walks in nature. Focus on the sights, sounds, and smells around you and allow your mind to relax and focus on creative thinking.

9. *Outdoor workspaces:* Set up an outdoor workspace with a comfortable desk and chair. If the weather

permits, you can move your work outside for a refreshing change of scenery.

10. *Seasonal creativity celebrations:* Align your creative projects with the changing seasons. Use seasonal elements, colors, and themes to bring variety and inspiration to your work.

CHAPTER ELEVEN

Words that Dance, Tales that Enchant

STORYTELLING TECHNIQUES IN OUR personal lives refer to the use of narrative elements and communication skills to convey information, experiences, or messages compellingly and engagingly. Humans are naturally drawn to stories, and incorporating storytelling techniques into our communication can improve our ability to connect with others, make ideas more memorable, and foster deeper understanding.

Think of life as a big book in which our stories are like special chapters. Sometimes our journey is full of happy moments, like the first time we got excited. But sometimes it's also difficult, for example when we have to say goodbye to someone important to us. Can you remember these moments?

Now we imagine the people in our stories — our friends, our family, and those we love. They are like characters in a book and leave behind memories that we can't forget. Think about the ups and downs that have made you stronger. Life is like a painting with bright colors of laughter and a few shades of tears. How do these colors make your story unique?

In simple words, let's share these stories as if we were talking around a cozy fire. Imagine feeling connected, as if you were talking to a friend. Can you feel the warmth in the words we share? Our stories are like magic — they can help us understand each other better. When we read together, we want to find out how each other's stories make a beautiful melody. How does your heart respond to the feelings we discover in these shared stories?

10 creative ways to approach storytelling techniques:

1. *Interactive Storytelling Workshops:* Host workshops where participants create a story together. This encourages collaboration and different perspectives.

2. *Digital storytelling:* Use multimedia elements such as images, audio, and video to enhance your narrative.

Create a dynamic and engaging experience for your audience.

3. *Story cubes or cards:* Use story dice or cards with images or prompts. Roll dice or draw cards at random to develop creative ideas for your story.

4. *Reverse storytelling:* Start with the conclusion or a critical moment in the story and work backward, revealing the details that led up to that point. This can create more tension and intrigue.

5. *Storytelling through art:* Combine storytelling with visual art. Illustrate key scenes or characters from your story to complement your oral narrative with a visual narrative.

6. *Storytelling in different genres:* Experiment with telling the same story in different genres, such as comedy, drama, or mystery. This exercise will help you try out different tones and styles.

7. *Storytelling with personal objects:* Ask participants to bring an object that has a personal meaning to them. Use these objects as inspiration to create unique stories and connect personal experiences to the narrative.

8. *Collaborative story mapping:* Create a large visual map of the story world on a whiteboard or poster. Ask

participants to add details and elements to the map as the story unfolds.

9. *Character interviews:* Conduct interviews with the characters in your story as if they were real people. This will help you better understand their motivations and personalities and enrich the storytelling process.

10. *Time travel storytelling:* Tell the story from different time perspectives — the past, the present, and the future. This unconventional approach makes your narrative more complex and multi-layered.

CHAPTER TWELVE

Inhale Serenity, Exhale Clarity

MINDFULNESS PRACTICES REFER TO a set of techniques and exercises aimed at cultivating a heightened state of awareness and presence in the present moment. These practices have their roots in ancient contemplative traditions such as Buddhism, but they have also gained popularity in various secular contexts such as psychology and wellness.

In our personal lives, mindfulness practices can have a profound impact on our mental, emotional, and physical well-being.

Think of life as a storybook where mindfulness is the gentle art of being in the present moment. It's as if you have a quiet garden within you where you can enjoy the beauty of the now without letting past regrets or future worries disturb you. See it as a special conversation with yourself in which you discover a serenity that is just waiting to become part of your daily life.

Mindfulness is like a comforting friend that helps you to look at your feelings without being too hard on yourself. Take a moment to breathe deeply — each breath is a chance to feel refreshed, like a promise of a new beginning. The words on these pages are like friendly lights to help you better understand your feelings.

This book is your companion in self-discovery. It gently invites you to explore the different parts of your own story. Can you recognize how important it is to be kind to yourself like a delicate flower opening up to the world? In this book, you don't just read words, you find a place where you connect with your own heart. It's an adventure where you become the author of your journey and create a story in which you're present, kind, and truly alive.

Here are some important aspects of mindfulness practice and their meaning:

1. *Mindfulness in the present moment:* Mindfulness encourages people to focus on the present moment without judgment. This includes

paying attention to thoughts, feelings, and sensations as they arise without getting too caught up in them.

2. *Reduce stress and anxiety:* Mindfulness has been proven to help reduce stress and anxiety. By being present and observing your thoughts without attachment, you can distance yourself from stressors and react more calmly to challenging situations.

3. *Better emotion regulation:* Mindfulness helps people develop a greater awareness of their emotions. This self-awareness can lead to improved emotion regulation, enabling people to respond to emotions in a more measured and constructive way.

4. *Better concentration and focus:* Regular mindfulness practice is associated with improved concentration and cognitive function. By training the mind to focus on the present moment, people find it easier to concentrate on tasks and make decisions.

5. *Increased self-awareness:* Mindfulness promotes self-reflection and self-awareness. It involves observing one's thoughts and behaviors without judging them, which leads to a deeper understanding of oneself and habitual thought patterns.

6. *Increased compassion and empathy:* Mindfulness practices often foster a sense of compassion, both for oneself and for others. By cultivating a

non-judgmental attitude, people can become more empathetic and understanding in their relationships.

7. *Better physical health:* There is evidence that mindfulness practices can have positive effects on physical health. These include lower blood pressure, improved immune function, and better sleep.

8. *Mind-body connection:* Mindfulness emphasizes the connection between the mind and the body. Practices such as mindfulness breathing and body awareness exercises help to tune into physical sensations and promote overall well-being.

Common mindfulness practices include mindfulness meditation, mindful breathing, body scan meditation, and mindful movement activities such as yoga or tai chi. Integrating these practices into everyday life can contribute to a more balanced and fulfilling life and promote a better sense of connection with oneself and the world.

10 creative ways to incorporate mindfulness practices into your everyday life:

1. *Mindful coloring:* Engage with adult coloring books and mindfully focus on each stroke and color choice. This is a calming and creative way to practice mindfulness.

2. *Take sensory walks:* Take a mindful walk and pay attention to your senses. Notice the textures, smells, and sounds around you. This promotes awareness of the present moment.

3. *Mindful eating ritual:* Turn a meal into a mindful experience. Pay attention to the taste, texture, and smells. Chew slowly and savor every bite without distraction.

4. *Creative journal writing:* Combine mindfulness with creativity by keeping a journal. Use words, drawings, or mixed media to express your thoughts mindfully and reflectively.

5. *Breathwork with art:* Create art while focusing on your breath. Breathe in and out consciously as you draw, paint, or craft. Let your breath guide the creative process.

6. *Nature meditation:* Go outside with your mindfulness. Sit quietly in nature, observe your surroundings, feel the wind, and listen to the sounds. Connect with the present moment in a natural environment.

7. *Mindful use of technology:* Practice mindfulness when using technology. Set aside specific times to check emails or social media and do so with full attention, noticing every action.

8. *Body scan meditation with movement:* Combine a body scan meditation with gentle movement. Pay attention to every part of your body as you move, fostering a mind-body connection.

9. *Creative breathing exercises:* Experiment with different breathing techniques, such as box breathing or pattern breathing, while engaging in a creative activity such as painting or writing.

10. *Art of gratitude:* Create a piece of art that represents the things you're grateful for. This mindful exercise not only promotes creativity but also a positive attitude.

CHAPTER THIRTEEN

Crafting Visionaries, Field by Field

FIELD-SPECIFIC CREATIVITY GENERALLY REFERS to the ability to develop creative ideas, solutions, or products in a particular field or area of expertise. This means that creativity isn't a uniform characteristic, but can be highly context-dependent. In our personal lives, domain-specific creativity can manifest itself in different ways depending on our interests, hobbies, and areas of expertise.

In the world of personal creativity, each of us has a special canvas on which to paint our passions and ideas. Imagine having a unique piece of paper on which you can draw or write about things you love. Imagine using bright colors to represent your interests and hobbies to make your canvas vibrant and colorful.

Now imagine this canvas as a magical place where you can create amazing things. But here's the interesting part: – As you explore and create, you might ask yourself a few questions. For example: What beautiful masterpiece can you make from the things you love to do? It's like asking yourself what fantastic picture you can paint on your special canvas.

When you work on personal projects, it's like weaving a story with your favorite colors and patterns. The projects become stories full of creativity and excitement. Here's a question: how do you make your everyday tasks extraordinary and turn them into something like a beautiful song?

Education and learning can be like an adventure. When you learn new things, you might ask yourself: What amazing discoveries can you make along the way? It's a bit like being an explorer in the world of knowledge and finding hidden treasures of wisdom.

Now think of technology and innovation. It's as if you're shaping the future with your clever ideas. How can you use your imagination to create something new and exciting, like building your version of the future?

The story of your creativity unfolds on these pages. It's not just about being good at something; it's about expressing yourself in a way that feels truly special. Your creativity is like a unique melody that makes life more colorful and meaningful. Let's go on a journey together where your ideas and passions can transform ordinary moments into something extraordinary.

Here are a few examples of how subject-specific creativity can be applied to personal life:

1. Hobbies and interests:

- If you have a passion for painting, your subject-specific creativity could be developing innovative techniques, styles, or concepts in the visual arts.

- In cooking, you might experiment with unique flavor combinations or forms of presentation.

2. Professional life:

- In your profession, subject-specific creativity means coming up with inventive solutions to problems in your industry or profession. This could mean creating new processes, improving existing processes, or developing innovative products or services.

3. Personal projects:

- If you're interested in DIY or craft projects, your subject-specific creativity might involve inventing new designs, using materials in novel ways, or creatively solving challenges in your projects.

4. Learning and education:

- If you are learning a new skill or studying a particular subject, your subject-specific creativity might be demonstrated in your ability to connect and apply knowledge in unique ways, perhaps solving problems or tackling issues in ways that others might not have thought of.

5. Technology and innovation:

- For tech enthusiasts, domain-specific creativity can mean programming, designing, or solving problems in ways that push the boundaries of what is currently possible in a particular technical field.

Essentially, domain-specific creativity is about combining your knowledge, skills, and experience to come up with new and valuable ideas in a particular area of interest or expertise. This allows you to stand out from the crowd and make a meaningful contribution to your field by adding a personal touch and innovative thinking to your efforts.

10 creative ways to foster discipline-specific creativity:

1. *Cross-industry collaboration:* Collaborate with professionals from other industries to bring new perspectives and ideas to your field.

2. *Inspiration from unlikely sources:* Draw inspiration from areas outside your industry, look for connections, and apply concepts in innovative ways.

3. *Reverse engineering:* Analyse successful solutions or products in your field and then reverse engineer them to find new approaches or improvements.

4. *Scenario planning:* Imagine future scenarios for your industry and come up with creative solutions to potential challenges or opportunities.

5. *Simulation and role-playing:* Use simulation exercises or role-playing to simulate real-life scenarios and encourage innovative problem-solving.

6. *Creative constraints:* Examine what constraints exist in your field and challenge yourself to find creative solutions within those constraints.

7. *Application of Design Thinking:* Apply the principles of design thinking to accurately understand the needs of

users or customers and develop solutions that meet those needs.

8. *Borrow analogies:* Find analogies from unrelated fields and apply them to solve problems or develop ideas in your area of expertise.

9. *Scenario exchange:* Share scenarios or challenges with professionals in other fields and propose solutions to encourage other perspectives.

10. *Technology integration:* Investigate how new technologies can be integrated into your field to streamline processes, improve experiences, or create new opportunities.

CHAPTER FOURTEEN

Ignite Your Spirit, Sculpt Your Story

PERSONAL GROWTH THROUGH CREATIVITY refers to the idea that engaging in creative activities can contribute significantly to a person's personal development and well-being. This concept encompasses various forms of self-expression, artistic endeavors, and innovative thinking.

Imagine life as a book in which there is a special chapter entitled *Personal Growth through Creativity*. This chapter is like a beautiful garden in which your personal development blossoms. Think of creativity as the magic that transforms ordinary moments into extraordinary moments.

Imagine you have a paintbrush, a musical instrument, or even just a pen and paper. These are your tools for self-discovery. Have you ever thought about how painting, making music, or writing can reveal your unique story? It's like opening a treasure chest full of feelings and dreams.

As you embark on this creative journey, ask yourself: What stories are hidden inside me, waiting to be told? Your creativity is a safe space where the whispers of your heart find a voice. It's as if you transform feelings into colors and words, expressing the beauty of your soul.

Creativity isn't only about creating beautiful things, but also about solving the puzzles of life. Have you ever thought about how being creative helps you figure things out and discover new sides of yourself? It's as if you have a superpower that turns challenges into adventures.

Think of the moments when you're completely immersed in drawing, writing, or crafting. Time seems to slow down and you find yourself in a peaceful state of mind. You know that calming feeling, like a gentle rain that washes away the stress?

Creativity also promotes important life skills, such as being strong in difficult times and believing in yourself. Can you hear the confidence and resilience growing within you, like a melody playing in the background of your life?

Life is a team effort, and creativity connects us. Imagine working with others, sharing ideas, and creating something together. Have you ever felt the joy of being part of a creative community where everyone contributes to a beautiful masterpiece?

As you turn the pages of your life, let creativity bring color and meaning to your story. Imagine the satisfaction and happiness as your unique journey unfolds, like a symphony of creativity echoing through the chapters of your life. Can you feel the fulfillment of being the author of your own creative story?

Here are some important aspects of how personal growth through creativity can manifest in our personal lives:

1. *Self-expression:* creative activities provide an outlet for self-expression. Whether in art, writing, music, or other forms of creativity, everyone can express their thoughts, feelings, and experiences in unique and personal ways.

2. *Problem-solving and innovation:* Creativity is about thinking outside the box and finding new solutions to challenges. Those who cultivate a creative mindset can improve their problem-solving skills and approach life's obstacles with an innovative perspective.

3. *Increased self-awareness:* Creative activities often require self-reflection and self-awareness. Through the creative process, people can gain insight into their values, beliefs, and aspirations, leading to improved self-awareness.

4. *Resilience and adaptability:* The creative process often brings setbacks and challenges. Learning to deal with these obstacles will strengthen your resilience and adaptability - valuable qualities that contribute to your personal growth and development.

5. *Mindfulness and flow:* Creative activities can induce a state of flow in which you focus entirely on the present moment and experience a deep sense of concentration and satisfaction. This state of mindfulness can help reduce stress and increase well-being.

6. *Build self-confidence:* When you successfully create something, whether it's a piece of art, a story, or a solution to a problem, it can boost your self-confidence. The feeling of accomplishment can be transferred to other areas of your life and encourages you to take on new challenges.

7. *Catharsis and emotional healing:* Creativity can serve as a kind of catharsis that allows people to process and release pent-up feelings. This emotional release can contribute to a sense of relief and healing.

8. *Continuous learning:* The creative process often involves the acquisition of new skills and knowledge. Continuous learning and skill development contribute to personal growth and a sense of fulfillment.

9. *Connecting with others:* Creative activities can provide opportunities for socializing and collaboration. Sharing creative work with others, participating in group activities, or collaborating on projects can foster a sense of community and common purpose.

10. *Life satisfaction:* Ultimately, personal growth through creativity can contribute to an increased sense of fulfillment and life satisfaction. The act of creating and creative expression can add meaning and purpose to one's life.

Incorporating creative activities into your daily life, be it writing, painting, playing an instrument, or other forms of expression, can have a very positive impact on your personal development.

10 creative ways to foster personal growth:

1. *Create a vision board:* Create a vision board that visually represents your personal and professional goals. Use images, quotes, and symbols to inspire and motivate you.

2. *Keep a creative journal:* Keep a creative journal where you not only write down your thoughts and experiences but also include sketches, doodles, and creative expressions. This process can help you reflect on your growth journey.

3. *Narrate your life:* Share your life experiences in the form of a personal narrative. Writing a story about your journey helps you understand your experiences and identify areas for growth.

4. *Mindful art practices:* Engage in mindful art activities such as drawing, painting, or sculpting. The process of mindful creation of art can promote self-discovery and stress reduction.

5. *Creative goal setting:* Set your personal and professional goals creatively. Instead of a traditional list, you can use visual representations or create a vision map that aligns with your goals.

6. *Creative problem-solving workshops:* Approach personal challenges as if they were design problems. Host creative problem-solving workshops for yourself where you brainstorm and experiment with innovative solutions.

7. *Expressive dance or movement:* Use dance or movement as a form of self-expression. This can help you connect with your feelings, relieve stress, and tap into your inner creativity.

8. *Personal branding through design:* Design a personal logo or brand identity that reflects your values and aspirations. This visual representation can serve as a reminder of your growth journey.

9. *Photo Voice Project:* Create a photo voice project where you take photos that represent different aspects of your life. Reflect on the meaning of each photo and how it impacts your personal growth.

10. *Collage of strengths and successes:* Create a collage that highlights your strengths, accomplishments, and moments of personal triumph. Hang this collage in a visible place to inspire you.

Thank You

DEAR READERS,

If you enjoyed my book, please consider leaving a review on Amazon.

Your feedback will help other readers find books they like and help me keep writing the stories you want to read.

To leave a review, simply go to your Amazon account and click on the "Write a review" button under the book title.

Thank you so much for your support!

Mail me at monalisa.panda@gmail.com

About The Author

ONALISA PATNAIK, AS AN author, blogger, and YouTuber, is dedicated to motivating her audience through educational content that promotes personal growth.

On her blog, Growth Ignites, she publishes insightful posts designed to inspire positive change. On her popular YouTube channel, she shares inspirational videos that inform and encourage viewers to actively improve their lives. She also puts her leadership skills into practice as the founder of the IT product and service company, Britechsoft. With her diverse experience, Monalisa is an influential voice guiding others on their -way to self-improvement across all platforms. Her passion is evident in the diverse work she does to motivate and inspire her audience.

About The Book

W HEN WE REACH THE final pages of "100 Creative Thinking Techniques", we find ourselves equipped with a treasure trove of tools to unlock the limitless potential of our imagination. Each technique has been a stepping stone that has guided us through the vast landscape of creativity and innovation. Armed with these insights, we now stand on the threshold of new possibilities.

Let's conclude by reflecting on the journey we have taken together. The book has guided us through the trials and tribulations of thinking and encouraged us to question, explore, and redefine the boundaries of our creativity. From brainstorming to mind mapping, from lateral thinking to reverse brainstorming, the techniques presented were the keys to opening the doors to innovative thinking. This exploration of creativity should not be an end, but a beginning.

The field of creativity is infinite, and the techniques presented here are not mere conclusions, but catalysts for further discovery. It is an invitation to continue the journey into the unexplored territories of our minds, and to be equipped with the confidence to tackle challenges with new perspectives.

Don't see this as the end, but the beginning of a lifelong practice of creative thinking. The book serves as a guide, but your creative journey is an ever-evolving narrative. Let the techniques learned here be the seeds that are planted in the fertile soil of your imagination and sprout into innovative solutions, breakthrough ideas, and a more creative life. As we close this chapter, let the spirit of creativity live on in your daily endeavors. Embrace the unknown, celebrate the unconventional, and continue to cultivate a mindset that sees opportunity in every challenge. The book will find its place on the shelf, but the echoes of creative thinking will reverberate in the decisions you make, the problems you solve, and the ideas you realize.

May your creative journey be an everlasting adventure, full of the joy of discovery and the satisfaction of turning the spark of imagination into tangible brilliance. Here's to the limitless potential of your creative spirit, always ready to innovate, inspire, and shape the world in unexpected ways.